Tuck-Me-In Talks

with Your Little Ones

Grace Fox

HARVEST HOUSE PUBLISHERS
EUGENE, OREGON

AUG 19 2014

Cover by Dugan Design Group, Bloomington, Minnesota

Cover photo © Dugan Design Group

Grace Fox is published in association with the literary agency of The Steve Laube Agency, LLC, 5025 N. Central Ave., #635, Phoenix, Arizona, 85012.

TUCK-ME-IN TALKS WITH YOUR LITTLE ONES

Copyright © 2014 by Grace Fox
Published by Harvest House Publishers
Eugene, Oregon 97402
www.harvesthousepublishers.com

ISBN 978-0-7369-5640-6 (pbk.)

ISBN 978-0-7369-5641-3 (eBook)

Printed in the United States of America

13 14 15 16 17 18 19 20 21 22 / BP-JH / 10 9 8 7 6 5 4 3 2 1

Take Time to Talk

We develop strong relationships with our youngsters by spending time with them. Both the quantity and the quality of these interactions are important. This calls for intentionality and creativity.

My husband and I raised three kids. As a family, we read books together, attended summer camps, and interacted through biking, boating, and playing board games. But we also made time to talk one-on-one—with no parental agenda. One way we did this was by asking simple questions at bedtime.

We began this tradition with our youngest child. Kimberly was in kindergarten at the time, and she loved this routine. Her answers—sometimes silly, sometimes more serious—gave us a glimpse into her mind. Her answers often prompted more questions, and the ensuing conversations established a strong connection between us.

I'm thrilled that you want to connect with your children too. As you use *Tuck-Me-In Talks with Your Little Ones*, you'll see that some questions are easier than others. They are designed to meet the needs of families with kids ages three to eight with a wide range of verbal skills. If a particular question doesn't resonate with one child, try a different one. That child might respond enthusiastically to the same question a few weeks later.

Some questions are educational, some are plain ol' silly, and some are spiritual. Listen to the answers and engage your youngsters with further questions. Laugh with them and explore with them. Children's imaginations change as they grow, so you'll be able to use *Tuck-Me-In Talks with Your Little Ones* over and over. Keep a notebook handy—you may wish to record the answers.

Use this resource in a way that best fits your family's needs. If bedtime doesn't work for you, use it at mealtime or when you're driving somewhere. The point is, use it to develop your relationship with your kids.

Grandparents, this works for you too. I have five grandchildren, ages five and under, and the oldest two ask me to read them these questions. Their answers always bring a smile to my face.

Enjoy this book and love your kids. Whoever said, "Enjoy them now because they'll be grown and gone before you know it" was right.

Cheering for you and your family,

Grace

www.gracefox.com

How do you think
ice cream is made?

What's your
favorite **flavor**?

What are your
favorite **toppings**?

What **clothes** do you like wearing **the most**?

Why do you like them **more** than your **other clothes**?

What's the best way
to eat **spaghetti**?

Ice cream?

Jell-O?

Show me a **sad face**.

Name **three** things
that make you **sad**.

Now show me a **happy face**.

Name **three** things
that make you **happy**.

Pretend you're an **astronaut** looking out the window of your **spaceship**.

What do you **see** out there?

How many **stars**?

How bright is the **sun**?

What does the **earth** look like?

What's your
favorite **game**?

Explain the **rules** to me.

Why do you like it
more than
other games?

Why are
fire engines
red?

Name **five**
other objects
that are
the **same color**.

God made
mother kangaroos
with a **front pocket** where
their **babies** can
snuggle and grow.

Their babies are
like a **treasure**.

What **treasure** do
you like to carry in
your **pockets**?

Let's think of
five ways we can
be **kind** to
grandmas
and
grandpas.

How do you think
doughnuts
are made?

If you were a **baker**,
what **toppings** would
you put on
doughnuts?

Name **five** farm animals
and make their **noises**.

Which one do
you like **best**?

Why?

Let's plan a pretend
birthday party.

How many **friends**
will you invite?

What **games** will you play?

What **decorations**
will you choose?

Describe the **cake**—
what does it **look like**
and how does it **taste**?

If you could build **a tree fort**, what would it **look like**?

What **materials** would you use to build it?

What **furniture** would you put inside?

How would you **climb** into it— using stairs, a ladder, a rope, or something else?

How does a **lemon** taste?

Tell me how to make
lemonade.

How could I make a
lemon pie?

What **frightens** you?

What do you do when
you **feel afraid**?

What other things can
you do when you
feel afraid?

Pretend you're in a **circus**!

What's **your job**?

Tell me what you do
all day.

Name five **vegetables**
and their **colors**.

Which one is your **favorite**?

How should we **cook** it?

Tell me about
a **good thing**
that happened to you
today.

Laugh a silly **laugh** for me.

What **three** things
make you **laugh**?

Make me **laugh**
by telling me a
funny joke!

Name **ten** things
God created.

I'm glad
He created **you**!

What's the **most fun** winter activity you've **enjoyed**?

What **new** winter activity would you **like to do**?

What's your favorite **song**?

Sing it for me!

If you could be a **wild animal**, which one would you **be**?

Where would you **live**?

What would you **eat**?

If you could do **anything** you wanted during summer vacation, **what** would you do?

Who would you do it with?

How is **pizza** made?

What **toppings**
do you think
make the best **pizza**?

What's your
favorite **Bible story**?

Tell it to me, please.

If you could have
any pet you wanted,
what would you have?

What would it **look** like?

What **name**
would you give it?

What's your favorite **color**?

Name **five** things
that are **this color**.

If you could **change**
one thing about
your **bedroom,**
what would you change?

Describe what
your ideal **bedroom**
would **look** like.

What activity
do you do **really** well?

I think you're
really good at...

What's your
favorite **chore**?

What's your
least favorite **chore**?

How can we
make it **more fun**?

What's our
telephone number?

What's our **street address**?

I'm **so glad** we share the
same phone number
and address!

Pretend you own a pet **elephant**.

Where does it **sleep** at night?

What do you **feed** it?

What is its **name**?

What **games** does it like to **play**?

If you could
play any musical instrument,
what would you play?

Why that instrument?

Show me how you'd play it.

What's your
favorite **movie**?

Who's your
favorite **character**?

Why do you
like **this** character
more than others?

Name **five** animals that
have either
stripes or **spots**.

Which one's
your **favorite**?

Why?

Who's your **best friend?**

What do **you**
like about **him** or **her?**

What does it mean
to **be kind**?

Let's list **three** kind things
we can do
for our **neighbors**.

Which one of those things
would you
like to do **first**?

Pretend you're a **cowboy**
who works on a **ranch**.

What **jobs** do you do **all day**?

How many **cows** do you have?

What do they **eat**?

What's the **name** of
your **horse**?

What does it **look** like?

What does it mean
to **be polite**?

What's the **polite** thing
to **say** if you want
your mom or dad to
do something for you?

What's the **polite** thing
to **say** if someone
gives you a **treat**?

What's a **fun activity**
you'd like to do
with your **mom**?

With your **dad**?

Pretend you're a **zookeeper**.

What **jobs** will you do **today**?

What's your favorite **animal** at the zoo?

Why is that one your favorite?

Oh-oh— a **monkey** just escaped from its **cage**!

How will you **catch** it?

What kind of **car**
    would you like to **drive**
  if you were old enough?

What **color** would it be?
            How many **people**
            would it hold?

Would you take **me**
  for a **ride**?

Where would you take me?

If you could write a **book**,
what would it be about?

What would the **title** be?

Tell me the story, please!

List **five** ways to
show **kindness** to
your friends if
they're **feeling sad**.

You're a **good friend**!

Pretend you're in
a **submarine**.

What do you **see** when you
look out its window?

Describe the **fish** you see.
How many are there?
What **colors** are they?

Describe the **smallest** fish.
The **biggest**. The **prettiest**.
The **ugliest**.

If
you
could have
your own
Christmas
tree, how would
you decorate it?
With **popcorn strands**?
Shiny **garlands**? Homemade
ornaments? Colored
lights
?

What's the
best part
about **Christmas**?

What's the best
Christmas present
you've ever **received**?

What's the best
Christmas present
you've ever **given**?

What does it mean
to **be patient**?

Why is **patience** important?

Tell me about a time
when you were not patient.

Tell me about a time
you were patient.

Name **five** or more **round** objects.

Which ones can you **eat**?

Which ones can you **play with**?

What can you do with **the rest**?

God made
ducks' feet special.

They can walk on ice
without getting cold!

What might happen
if we walk on ice
with **bare feet**?

Pretend you drive a **big truck**.

What do you
haul in the trailer?

Where are you
taking the load?

What do you **see**
as you drive down the road?

What's your favorite **TV show?**

Why do you like it so much?

Who's your favorite **character?**

What's a **baby bear** called?

A **baby dog**?

Pig?

Goose?

Fox?
(*A baby fox is a kit*)

I wonder why God made **ladybugs**.

What do you think?

Why did He make **spiders**?

Describe the **most unusual bug** you've ever seen.

List **five** words
that start with the letter *L*.

I know a
very important *L* word!

Can you **guess** what it is?

Love!

I love you **very much**.

Pretend you're a **snowman**.

What are you
wearing on your **head**?

What are your **eyes**, **nose**,
and **mouth** made of?

Oh-oh,
the sun is shining now.

Can you **show me**
what's happening to **you**?

List **five** words
that begin with *B*.

Now make **a sentence**
in which every word
begins with *B*.

Do the same
with the letters
D and *M*.

What do you think
Mommy does all day?

What does **Daddy** do?

Did you know that **dolphins**
sleep with one eye **open**
and one eye **closed**?

Giraffes sleep **standing up**.
They keep both eyes **open**,
and they **wiggle** their ears.

Why do you think God made
them to sleep this way?
(So they can escape quickly if an enemy comes.)

Show me how you sleep.

Name **five** words
that begin with
    the letter *S*.

        I know a word that
        begins with *S—special*!

Name **three** things
    you think are **special**.

Pretend you're an **artist** who **paints pictures** to hang in people's houses.

Describe your favorite **painting**.

What does it **look** like?

What **colors** did you use?

Show me an **angry** face.

What makes you feel **angry**?

What makes that
angry feeling **go away**?
(Tickle time!)

Why do **babies cry**?

What makes them **stop**?

What makes **you** cry?

What makes you **stop**?

Finish this sentence:

I wish I could go to...

Why did you choose that place?

Pretend it's a hot, **hot** day.

How can you stay **cool**?

What **activity** would
you like to do?

What **snack** or **drink**
do you want?

What **job** would
you like to have when
you're a **grown-up**?

What things would
you do **all day**?

If your **best friend** invited
you to his or her
birthday party,
what **gift** would you take?

Why did you choose
this **gift**?

What
would you
buy
if you had
one dollar
to spend
?

How does a **kangaroo** move
from place to place?
A **snake**?

A **fish**?

A **bird**?

What are some of the ways
you can **move**
from one place to another?

Let's count
from one to twenty
forward
and then **backward**
together.

Now it's **your turn**
to do it
on your own!

How **strong** is **God**?

Show me with your muscles!

What **problems**
do you think **God**
can help you **solve**?

I **wonder** why God made **mommies**.

What do **you** think?

Tell me about a time
when you **shared** something
with someone.

How did that make you **feel**?

When you share things,
I feel proud of you!

Let's sing
"**Jesus Loves Me**"

and then **thank** Him

for **loving us** so much.

If you could spend
an **afternoon**
        riding your **bike**,
reading a **book**,
        swimming at the **pool**,
or playing computer **games**,

which would you **choose**?

                    Why?

How do **butterflies taste** food?
(*They taste with their feet!*)

If you were a **butterfly,** what foods would you like to **taste** with your **feet**?

What do you think a **sidewalk** would **taste** like?

Pretend you saw
someone drop some **money**
on the ground
without noticing.

What should you **do**?

Psalm 147:4 says that
God has named **every star**
in the sky.

If you could name
five stars,
which **names**
would you **choose**?

How is an **eagle** different
from a **hummingbird**?

How is a **dandelion** different
from an **apple tree**?

How is a **lion** different
from a **squirrel**?

How are **you** and **I**
different from each other?

How are we the **same**?

Jesus says we should **pray** for other people.

Who would you like to **pray** for now?

What would you like to **ask God** to do for him or her?

What's the **best part** about **waking up** in the morning?

I think the best part
about waking up is...

Here are **five** reasons why
I love you.

Whom do you love?

Can you think of
five reasons **why**?

God helps us
do many things.

Let's list things we can do
with His help, beginning each
sentence with "**I can**."

For example,
  "**I can** brush my teeth.
  I can ride a bike."

Name **five** fruits
and their **colors**.

What's your
favorite fruit?

How is a
fruit **smoothie**
made?

What **plants** would
you choose if you
 could grow your
own **garden**?

How would you
help them **grow well**?

Guess how many **bones** God put in an **owl's neck**.
(*Fourteen! Humans have seven.*)

I wonder why He did that.

What do **you** think?
(*Owls need to turn their necks many directions because their eyes don't move.*)

Pretend you're an **owl**— hold your eyes still and turn your head so you can see where you're walking.

If you were
king of the world,
what **rules** would you
tell everyone to **obey**
?

Some children own very few **toys**. Some own **none** at all!

If you had only **one toy**, what would it be?

If someone who had **no toys** came to your house to play, what **toy** would you **give** him or her?

The Bible says that
God knows
everything about us.

He knows
how many **hairs**
are on our heads, and
He knows
when we **wake up** and
when we **fall asleep**.

What else does
He know about us?

What does it
mean to be
thankful?

Let's thank God
for as many things
as we can.

How are
**chocolate chip
pancakes**
made
?

God says we're to
be **generous**.

What does that mean?

How can we be **generous**
to people who do not
have as many things
as we do?

Can you list
three
of our family's
safety rules
?

God says children are
to **obey** their **parents**.

Why is that so **important**?

What family rules are
hard for you to **obey**?

Pretend you're going to a **sleepover**.

What things will you **pack** in your suitcase?

Let's try to **name**
one animal for
every letter
of the alphabet.

Which ones are **good pets**?

Which ones are **not**?

Create three wacky
super-sandwiches.

What kind of
bread would you use?

What **fillings** would you use?

Which one would
you **like most**?

Why?

How many **arms** did
God give the **octopus**?

Their **arms** have no **bones**—
what do you think
that **feels** like?

If you had **eight arms**,
what would you **do** with them?

What does it mean
to **love someone**?

Think of **three** ways
we **show people** that
we **love** them.

Let's pretend
we're going to **invent a toy**.

What will this toy **look** like?

What fun things will it **do**?

How much will it **cost**?

Jesus says we can
talk to Him anytime,
day or night.

What
would you like
to tell Him
or ask Him
right now?

Finish this sentence:

I wish I could buy a...

Why did you choose
that wish?

God made **camels**
with **special eyes**
so **sand** can't blow into them.
(They have three eyelids!)

What did God do to
protect **our eyes**?
(He made us with eyelids,
eyelashes, and eyebrows.)

Jesus says that **heaven** is a **wonderful place**.

What do you think **heaven** is like?

Do you know how to **get to heaven**?

The Bible says that
God sends **angels**
to keep us **safe**.

What do you think
an angel **looks** like?

Grace Fox is a speaker at women's events internationally. To book her for your next retreat or conference, visit her website:
www.gracefox.com

Or email her at:
grace@gracefox.com

You can also follow Grace on her blog:
www.gracefox.com/blog

Or on Twitter:
@gracelfox

Or on Facebook:
www.fb.com/gracefox.author

More Great Harvest House Books from Grace Fox

10-Minute Time Outs for You and Your Kids
Grace provides engaging stories, activities, and prayers in a welcoming format to help you and your children share the riches of God's Word together.

Moving from Fear to Freedom
Grace demonstrates how you can face your fear and actually let it be a catalyst for change. She outlines "the upside of fear": When we stop hiding from God and instead cry out to Him for help, He answers, and we experience Him in new ways.

Peaceful Moments to Begin Your Day
In this lovely padded hardcover, Grace invites you to delight in your faith by nurturing your relationship with God each day. In these encouraging devotions, you will encounter inspirational stories, Scripture-based prayers, and engaging meditations that lead you to the grace, comfort, and wisdom of God's presence.

Morning Moments with God
Discover fresh biblical insights and renew your spirit as you savor more than 150 new devotions for women from Grace. These gems of godly wisdom focus on God's faithfulness and reflect on His power, presence, and promises in your life today.

To learn more about Harvest House books
or to read sample chapters, visit our website:
www.HarvestHousePublishers.com

HARVEST HOUSE PUBLISHERS
EUGENE, OREGON